Tus cinco sentidos y tu sexto sentido | Your Five Senses and Your Sixth Sense

La intuición: el sexto sentido

Intuition: The Sixth Sense

Clara Reade

Traducción al español: Eida de la Vega

PowerKiDS press.

New York

Published in 2014 by The Rosen Publishing Group, Inc.
29 East 21st Street, New York, NY 10010

First Edition

Editor: Jennifer Way and Amelie von Zumbusch
Book Design: Kate Vlachos
Photo Research: Katie Stryker

Traducción al español: Eida de la Vega

Photo Credits: Cover Flying Colours Ltd/Digital Vision/Getty Images; p. 4 altanaka/Shutterstock.com; p. 7 Anastasia Shilova/Shutterstock.com; p. 8 kedrov/Shutterstock.com; pp, 11, 24 (uneasy) Pavel L Photo and Video/Shutterstock.com; p. 12 Andrew L/Shutterstock.com; pp. 15, 19 iStockphoto/Thinkstock; p. 16 Hemera/Thinkstock; p. 20 KidStock/Blend Images/Getty Images; p. 23 Fuse/Thinkstock; p. 24 (brain) leonello calvetti/Shutterstock.com; p. 24 (danger) Ryan McVay/Photodisc/Thinkstock.

Library of Congress Cataloging-in-Publication Data

Reade, Clara.
  Intuition : The sixth sense = la intuición : el sexto sentido / by Clara Reade ; translated by Eida de la Vega. — First edition.
    pages cm. — (Your five senses and your sixth sense = tus cinco sentidos y tu sexto sentido)
  English and Spanish.
  Includes index.
  ISBN 978-1-4777-3280-9 (library)
  1. Intuition—Juvenile literature. I. Vega, Eida de la, translator. II. Reade, Clara. Intuition. III. Reade, Clara. Intuition. Spanish.
IV. Title. V. Title: Intuición.
  BF315.5.R42518 2014
  153.4'4—dc23

2013022581

Websites: Due to the changing nature of Internet links, PowerKids Press has developed an online list of websites related to the subject of this book. This site is updated regularly. Please use this link to access the list: www.powerkidslinks.com/yfsyss/intuit

Manufactured in the United States of America

CPSIA Compliance Information: Batch #W14PK3: For Further Information contact Rosen Publishing, New York, New York at 1-800-237-9932

CONTENIDO

CONTENTS

4

La intuición es un
presentimiento.
Reside más que nada
en tu **cerebro**.

Intuition is a gut feeling.
However, it mostly uses
your **brain**.

La intuición se asocia al lado derecho del cerebro.

People link it to the right side of the brain.

La gente le dice "el sexto sentido". El oído, la vista, el tacto, el gusto y el olfato son los otros sentidos.

People call it the sixth sense. Hearing, sight, touch, taste, and smell are the other senses.

La palabra "intuición" viene del latín.

The word "intuition" comes from Latin.

11

En japonés se le dice *chokkan*.

Chokkan is the Japanese word for it.

13

La intuición te advierte
si estás en **peligro**.

It warns you if you are
in **danger**.

15

Si te sientes **intranquilo**, ¡ten cuidado!

If you feel **uneasy**, be careful!

17

La intuición te ayuda a distinguir el bien del mal.

It helps you tell right from wrong.

La ética es el estudio
del bien y el mal.

Ethics is the study of right
and wrong.

¿Qué te dice tu intuición?

———————————————————

What does your intuition
tell you?

22

23

PALABRAS QUE DEBES SABER / WORDS TO KNOW

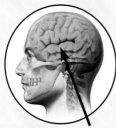

(el) cerebro
brain

(el) peligro
danger

intranquilo
uneasy